MESSIAH NON GRATA

musings of a madman

W0038624

By Scott T. Behr

Copyright 2022

All rights reserved

Paperback ISBN: 978-1-66786-328-3
eBook ISBN: 978-1-66786-329-0

THIS PAGE INTENTIONALLY LEFT BLANK

Everything,

Everything,

Everything, is Connected.

Like a spider's web.

SMM

To my children, grandchildren, and all that follow.

You are the light of my life.

About the author…

Just a regular guy.

By the way,

Scott T. Behr is not my real name.

Thank you to Christian, Elizabeth, and Roxsan for your

Help in the editing of this book.

The check's in the mail.

And thank you to spell checker,

You are a life savor.

About this book…

I am not a writer.

Please excuse any grammatical, or other errors.

This is my first book.

This is my last book.

If you like it,

Good.

If not,

Still good.

Read it at your leisure.

Have fun with it.

Think for yourself.

None of this will be on the test.

My original intention for this book

Was to provide my children

With an insight into my understanding

Of this life,

As I have found it to be.

And hopefully help them through this life,

And pass their knowledge on to their children, and so on.

We are all too busy to

Sit around discussing these things,

And I don't want to miss anything important.

So I put it in writing.

I then decided that there may be

Others out there that will find it helpful.

So I published it.

It is different than other books I've read.

It is more like bullet points than

Long, wordy paragraphs.

I try to cut through the crap.

It's sort of like a long poem.

A long poem with no rhyme

Or reason!!!

More like a list of ideas.

You fill in the blanks yourself.

Like that, you think about things for yourself.

Instead of just taking in what I say.

Because,

When it's all said and done,

All that matters is

What you think.

The topics will seem varied

And disjointed.

That is because this is a complex

System in which we live.

This civilization is a system.

A system created by humans.

Very intelligent humans,

Very long,

Long,

Long ago.

With their knowledge of the human psyche;

They were able to control the masses

Down through the ages by

Passing the knowledge down through

Their children and other select initiates.

There is nothing magical or mystical about it.

There are no chapters or page numbers.

It is formatted more to my way of thinking:

Everything all at once.

You see,

By nature, we think spatially.

Not

Linearly.

Have you ever noticed

How difficult it is to get young children

To keep their mind on one thing at a time?

It's not ADD or ADHD!!!

They seem to be all over the place.

Jumping from one thought to another.

Constantly.

It seems to take about 12 years of education,

And sometimes medication,

To condition us to think in a

Simple linear manner.

Furthermore,

We are conditioned to think in

Words.

I once had a teacher

Who learned English as a second language;

Say that;

You know when you <u>really</u> understand a language?

When you begin

Thinking in that language.

I would go further and say:

You really know how to <u>think</u>

When you think in <u>no</u> language at all.

Words limit our thinking,
And our ability to express our thoughts and ideas,
Depending on the length and depth of
The vocabulary we have learned.

Just like mathematics can only approximate infinity;
Not define it;
Words can only approximate our ideas, emotions,
Feelings, etc.

Did you ever find yourself saying,
"I can't seem to put it into words"?
Or,
"Je ne sais quoi"?

Did you ever see a cartoon character
When they get an idea?
A light bulb goes off above their head.

Have you ever noticed

You sometimes get an idea that seems to come from

Nowhere?

You think with your mind.

Your brain is just a biological organ

Like other organs; heart, kidneys, lungs, etc.

Your brain is like the motherboard of a computer.

It's where all the wires lead

For information to be organized and distributed.

Biologically,

Your brain is like

That of a dog, cat, etc.

Why can't dogs and cats learn more than simple tricks?

Perhaps, instead,

I should ask why they can't learn algaebra;

But I can't learn algabruh, either.

Hell, I can't even spell agleabra!!!

I doubt dogs and cats sit and wonder about the meaning of life.

But,

We do.

Unlike any other creature in this world,

We have a mind.

I can only explain it this way:

The mind is the combination of all;

Spirit,

Soul, and our physical

Body.

Are we god's creatures?

We are God.

NO BEGINNING

You have been lied to all of your life.

Don't believe me?

Your priest, pastor, reverend, shaman, witch doctor,

Guru, etc.

Have all been lying to you and everyone else

All your life and all through history.

Always having a hand out for donations.

Supposedly so they can help others and yourself.

You think they work as hard as you do?

It's not entirely their fault.

Afterall,

You give them authority over you.

Your politicians, officials, etc.

Have all been lying to you and everyone else

All your life and all through history.

Always having a hand out for taxes, fines, and fees.

Supposedly so they can help others and yourself.

You think they work as hard as you do?

It's not entirely their fault.

Afterall,

You give them authority over you.

Your parents, grandparents, aunts, uncles, etc.

Have all been lying to you and everyone else

All your life and all through history.

Always telling you to respect your elders, respect

Authority…

You think they know better than you do?

It's not entirely their fault.

Afterall,

Their parents taught them.

Working hard,

Scratching and scraping to save for that retirement.

Do you really think it will be there when you need it?

Severe economic depressions have been brought about

Throughout history.

During depressions

Money becomes scarce.

People lose their fortunes.

The money has to go somewhere.

Where?

Not with you or I.

You think you're immune?

Since the early 1990's the money supply has been

Expanded like never before.

However, there was no significant price inflation as a

Result.

How can that be?

Is this a "new" economy?

Somehow economic rules no longer apply?

At the same time almost all of the manufacturing in the
U.S. has gone to other countries.
Other countries with workers working for slave wages.

The prices of these products actually fell,
While the money supply expanded.

Therefore, no significant price inflation
Was noted.
Increased money supply and lower prices,
Due to cheap foreign labor,
Cancelled each other out.

At the same time,
The prices of real estate and stocks
Have exploded.

The prices of real estate and stocks
Are not counted in the
Price inflation figures.

Along with the vast expansion

Of the money supply,

Fewer dollars were needed for most purchases

Due to the lower prices of

Goods and services.

So, the extra money had to go somewhere;

So, it flowed to

Real estate and stocks;

Driving up their prices.

Can this go on forever?

Is there a breaking point?

You think you are safe holding gold and silver?

Gold and silver do have practical uses in manufacturing

And industry.

But their main function is still as a store of wealth.

A currency.

A curren(t)cy.

My name is Scott.

I am a recovering gold bug.

Is it possible the value of gold and silver could be

Manipulated as easily as that of the fiat dollar?

Platinum used to be twice the price of gold.

Now it's half.

A bank is the land on both sides along a river.

The river meanders as the banks guide it.

The river flows.

A flowing river has a current.

If you manipulate the bank,

You effect the current.

Banks manipulate the curren(t)cy.

What about cryptocurrencies?

Imaginary money.

Linked in cyberspace.

Constantly changing in value.

"Mined" using mathematical algorithms.

Created by "who knows who" and for

What purpose?

Don't get me started!!!

Pay your taxes,

Or go to prison.

Honest economists will admit federal income taxes are

Not needed to run the country.

The country ran for over a hundred years before federal

Income taxes.

Wars, roads, bridges, etc. were all paid somehow.

Federal income taxes started at about the same time as

The Federal Reserve System (Bank).

They knew they would eventually introduce a fiat

Monetary system.

They had a time table.

They plan things decades, centuries, or more in advance.

They are not stupid.

Their intention was a massive expansion in the
U.S. (and world) economy in the coming century.

As an aside:

Who are the THEY?

The "Real Rulers":

They are the people who have

Ruled the world farther back

Then we can possibly know.

You know.

The few people

Who make up the capstone of

The pyramid.

The real rulers stay behind the scenes.

We will never know their names.

Unlike their minions,

The real rulers are not obsessed with fame.

They only use money to control others.

Money really has no other meaning to them,

Because they rule and control ALL nations,

Governments, political parties, movements,

Religions, organizations, news media,

Entertainment media, education systems, etc.

Their control is all pervasive and trickles down to

All of us.

They know if the masses ever wised up,

Those at the top might become targets.

So, they have their minions as

Their front men.

These minions are the lesser rulers;

Kings, Queens, Presidents, Politicians,

High level bureaucrats, etc.

These minions understand the workings of the
System;

Either by being let into the secret, or by figuring

It out for themselves by observing how things

Really work behind the scenes.

They decide to "go along with it".

Choosing fame and fortune by being

The slave masters of the little people

For their masters: The Real Rulers.

The usual targets of conspiracy theorists:

The masons?

The trilaterals?

The committee of 300?

And so on???

These are just some of the organizations

For the workers that are used at times

To further their agenda.

The usual conspiracy theories mistakenly

Point to one or two of these organizations as being

The real rulers of the world.

The reason they have this simplistic view is that:

To believe the real truth

Leads one to feel hopeless.

Everyone wants a happy ending.

Like in the movies,

The bad guys lose in the end;

Everybody learns the truth;

The hero who was once castigated,

Is now justified.

The world is saved.

The truth is;

There is no white knight.

The masses will never learn the truth.

You will never be justified for your beliefs

By the masses.

Not even by your friends and family.

It's difficult to learn an ultimate truth

Like how things really work;

And not try to explain it to your friends and family.

You do it because you care for them.

You want to yell it from the rooftops!!!

The truth is,

Very few people can accept the truth.

Even though they have a feeling that what you

Are telling them is true.

Somehow, they feel that they have always known

It; but never <u>realized</u> it.

But to believe it would mean

Not being accepted by others.

So they continue to lie to themselves.

They put it out of their minds,

So they can get "back on track"

With "right thinking" as they have been taught.

If you do try to explain it to others;

You will probably become "one of those guys";

Like me.

You may notice you are no longer

Invited to as many parties or family gatherings

As you once were.

You become lumped in with all the

Nutty conspiracy theorists out there.

People start to prejudge your beliefs according to

The beliefs of others.

You become that crazy uncle or friend of the
Family everybody tolerates and laughs at behind
His back.
No one takes you seriously anymore.
Even if you are just talking about the weather,
They are expecting you to bring up chemtrails or
Secret weather modification technology;
Whether you agree with those things are not.
To them, you are and always will be, a
Conspiracy theorist.

So, I have found that sometimes it is necessary
To outwardly be neutral on topics other people
Speak to you about.
You know,
Go along to get along.
But, inside, always be true to yourself.
It's sort of like being an actor playing a part.

In your outward life you must live a lie

In order to "fit in".

But, inside, you know the truth.

This economic expansion was meant to fund a

Massive advancement of technology.

Don't believe me?

Look at the technological advancements

During the past century,

Compared to anytime in

Known human history.

Why are THEY obsessed with advanced technology?

Think about it.

If you were born into a very small class of people

Who control the world,

What would your life be like?

You would have anything you desired.

Anything you desired.

The only worry you would have is that it will end.

You know this physical body you were born into

Will die someday.

And ALL this will end.

You would become obsessed with

Extending your physical life

For as long as possible.

You, and the others of your class,

Would do everything possible to

Find a way to extend this physical life

Indefinitely.

Not just to add years to life,

But to add quality years.

Make 200 the new 20.

Don't get excited.

Believe me,

They will not give us this technology.

They will keep it a secret.

They will use it for themselves,

And dangle it as a carrot for their high

Level minions.

After all,

With all of the known medical advancements of the past

Century,

The average life span of men in the U.S.

Has gone from about 60 years to 78 years in the past

100 years.

For most people,

The last 15 years, or so, are spent suffering

With illnesses, chronic pain, and infirmities.

The previous 60 years (from about 1860) saw a life

Expectancy go from

40 years to about 60 years.

And the previous 100 years to that, saw a life expectancy

Go from 35 years to 40 years.

So,

Using rounded numbers (and a little aljibrah),

It took a quarter of a millennium

To little more than double our life span.

It's an increase of 120% in about 250 years.

But of that 120%,

The past century has only seen an

Increase of 30%.

That's only 30%, considering all of the

Medical and technological advancements <u>we know of</u>

In the past 100 years.

And,

I won't dare get into the skyrocketing cost of our

Medical care in the past century.

I once heard a doctor interviewed on a radio program

Explain that 200 years ago, and longer, if you lived past

The age of about 10 years, you had a significantly high

Chance of living to a ripe

Old age of about the mid 50's to mid 60's.

It's because high infant and childhood mortality rates

Brought the average life expectancy age down.

Remember,

Benjamin Franklin was 70 years old at the time of the

Declaration of Independence.

He lived to be 84.

This doctor further explained that the main factors

Credited for the increase in

Life expectancy for the past century were things like

Penicillin, clean water, good hygiene, and refrigeration.

What???

You mean with modern things like nuclear medicine,

Sophisticated types of imaging, gene therapy, mapping of

The human genome, chemo-therapy, countless new

Medications, organ transplants,

Hospitals that are larger than small cities, etc.;

We really owe our 18 years' extended life span to:

Penicillin, clean water, good hygiene, and

Refrigeration???

Have they reached the point of technological

Advancements

They yearned for?

Can THEY now extend their physical lives, indefinitely?

What happens now?

Do THEY really need so many people on this planet

To do the work for them anymore?

Ever noticed the skyrocketing cancer rates?

Is covid a test run for a more deadly

Pandemic?

Is it a coincidence they are always crying about

Over population?

"Mother Earth cannot support all of us"

Why would they want to save our lives

If there are too many of us?

I don't see any of them committing suicide to bring down

The population figures.

Now,

Getting back to their plans to massively

Expand the economy.

Gold and silver are constantly being mined;

However, their increase in supply is still constrained by

The rate at which they are being mined.

Stores of gold and silver have a finite supply.

In order to massively expand the economy, more

Money must be put into the hands of

The little people.

So,

Those with money must give up

A portion of

Their supply of money.

Can't have that!!!

Instead,

A fiat monetary system was introduced.

This is money with no intrinsic value.

It only has value

Because those in charge tell us so.

We are forced to accept it as payment

Because the government says it is

"Legal tender for all debts, public and private".

This fiat monetary system allows the rulers of the world

To run economies with money that

Costs nothing to produce

Without them having to give up any

Real wealth of their own.

A fiat monetary system needs constraints to

Control the flow of curren(t)cy.

Increase the money supply too much,

You end up with hyperinflation.

Federal income tax is one method used to control the Money supply.

Limit your disposable income (increase taxes).

Limit your ability to buy stuff.

The result is a limit on demand for products and services.

Thus, price inflation is kept in check.

<u>That is the real reason we have federal income taxes!!!</u>

As an aside;

The reason gold and silver

Have been used throughout history

As a medium of exchange,

Is because they are scarce and durable.

But mainly because gold coins resemble the sun;

And silver coins resemble the moon.

Mankind has always looked to "heaven"

For his god;

Go(l)d???

Ah, government.

The word government derives from the Latin language.

The language of the Ancient Roman Empire.

Govern means to control.

Ment means mind.

Government = Mind Control

Your mind controls your thoughts,

Thus, your actions.

Republican?

Democrat?

Socialist?

Communist?

Liberal?

Conservative?

Fascist?

Capitalist?

I have not voted in almost a decade.

And I never will again.

Stupid?

Voting means you have a say in who and how
Government is run.
Right?

> *A brief example of government's logic follows:*
> *When I was younger*
> *I worked a few short years for the*
> *Federal government.*

> *Once they sent me to a week-long class on*
> *Total Quality Management.*
> *Which, in essence, means*
> *Putting management duties on lower*
> *Level employees,*
> *So that they can cut the higher paying*
> *Middle management jobs.*

Anyway,

Their main theme was;

Do more with less by thinking out of the box.

They spent a week giving us rules on

How to think out of the box.

Rules…

On how to think,

Out of the box!!!

Everyone seems concerned about the nation's budget
Deficit.

A balanced budget has rarely happened since the
Introduction of a fiat monetary system.

A budget refers to the income and expenses for one
Year.
One year only.

A budget deficit means you spend more in one year than

You collect

In that same year.

Not to be confused with

The national debt.

This is the <u>total</u> money the federal government owes.

Trillions and trillions...

The cumulative debt.

Not just for one year.

Forget the national debt.

It is impossible for the federal government to have zero

Debt in a fiat monetary system.

The federal government issuing bonds (borrowing)

Is how money is introduced into the economy.

How does that work?

The U.S. Treasury issues bonds,

The Federal Reserve "creates" dollars (Federal Reserve

Notes)

By typing numbers on a keyboard,

And purchases those bonds from the Treasury.

Now the federal government has Federal Reserve Notes

To spend into the economy.

The Federal Reserve then trades those bonds

On the open market to investors depending on

Their (the Federal Reserve's)

Needs for controlling the money supply.

They buy more bonds in the open market,

When they want to release more

Money into the economy (bond prices increase = interest

Rates decrease).

This is called an "easy money" policy.

Conversely, the Federal Reserve sells bonds in the open

Market

When they want the economy to contract (bond prices

Decrease = interest rates increase).

This is called a "tight money" policy.

We haven't heard a peep about a

Tight money policy in the past 30 years.

At least,

Not at the time of this writing.

Yes,

No matter what anyone tells you;

This "free market economy"

Is actually a "centralized, planned economy".

Pay off the national debt:

All the money,

All the money,

All the money in the economy ends up

In the hands of the holders of U.S. government bonds.

There would be no money left for people like us.

This would be a depression like never seen before.

Have you ever really noticed your federal income taxes

Decrease?

I mean; have you noticed?

Forget what the media and politicians tell you.

Look at your pay check.

Don't pay attention to that man behind the curtain.

At the end of each president's term,

They always brag about decreasing taxes and balancing

The budget.

The budget they are talking about runs for several years

Into the future.

It is never actually put into effect.

That is;

It takes place several years into the next administration.

The budget they present is just numbers on a piece of

Paper,

Dreamed up by making unrealistic economic

Assumptions

That they know will never come true.

The next administration does not care what the previous

President's budget says.

They continue to increase the debt.

No matter what political party they belong to.

How could they possibly balance the budget at the same

Time as decreasing taxes?

Anyone with a mind knows this is just lies.

So…

Getting back to voting.

Or not voting.

I still believe the U.S. is the best country to live in at this

Point in time.

Not because of our "leaders".

But, in spite of them.

I won't go through the good things about this country.

You know those already.

After all;

Everyone likes to see a train wreck.

If it bleeds it leads.

I registered to vote in 1988, at 18.

The registrar of voters came to my

High school to sign us up.

Parents, teachers, and society in general said it is

Necessary.

After all, only in our country do people have the right

(Power) of self-determination. Right???

So I began voting.

I never missed an election.

I did this for about 25 years.

I never noticed a change for the better.

My taxes never decreased.

No laws to benefit me were ever passed.

I kept hearing the same complaints from everyone.

It's the Republicans… It's the Democrats…

It's the conservatives… It's the liberals…

If only our guys could win a majority,

Everything would be fine!!!

When their guys did get a majority,

It was still the same old story.

Nothing for the better happened.

The blaming just went on and on.

By the way;

Did you ever notice the bickering among politicians in the

Media over a particular bill in congress?

It seems like the arguments last for weeks on one or two

Particular pieces of legislation.

It seems like they are not getting anything done.

Misdirection?

Do you realize that every day the media covers these

Controversies,

Laws are being passed?

That's right;

Legislators legislate.

Their reason for existence is to make laws.

Every day they are in session;

Laws are being passed.

Will there ever be enough laws?

What are all these laws?

Why doesn't the media tell us?

After all,

Isn't the media there to "inform" us?

They sure are.

Just like a form is used when shaping wet concrete.

They shape and mold our thoughts and opinions

IN the FORM they want.

The government does have a website

Listing these laws.

Even so,

It takes teams of lawyers to write these laws.

Do you think you or I can comprehend them?

It doesn't matter.

You are forced to follow these laws.

Whatever they say they mean.

Or go to prison.

Don't think.

Just do as you're told.

That is self-determination?

By the way,

Do you know that federal congressmen can pass secret

Laws?

That's right.

These are laws regarding national security.

Or so we are told.

Or so we are not told.

So...

Which laws are secret?

Well,

That's a secret.

What laws affecting us, are we not allowed to know

About?

Well, you see, it's illegal for anyone to tell us.

It's illegal for them to tell what secret laws exist.

Not just what's in the law or what it means,

But, the very fact the law exists is illegal to reveal.

Self-determination on steroids?

In the Soviet Union,

It was a law

That all adults

Must vote.

Why?

Voting gives people the illusion they have a say so.

It's like a pressure relief valve.

If their guy doesn't win this time,

He will in another 4 or 8 years.

Then everything will be fine.

Right???

I personally know people that have ended relationships

With friends and family;

Because of a difference in opinion over politics.

Voting means giving authority over yourself to others.

Why?

Who are they?

What makes them so special?

I suppose because they lie well enough to fool the

Majority of voters.

The real rulers of the world have an agenda.

The agenda <u>WILL</u> move forward.

No matter how you vote.

The agenda <u>WILL</u> move forward.

No matter who is in office.

The agenda <u>WILL</u> move forward.

No matter what they tell us.

So;

Get Out The Vote???

Ah, religion.

Don't get me wrong.
I don't mean to criticize any particular religion.
I mean to criticize <u>ALL</u> of them.

<u>ALL</u> religions are man-made.

The word religion derives from Latin.
It basically means "to bind".

Religions bind your mind.
Your mind controls your thoughts
And, thus, your actions.

In the book of Romans in the bible it says that
The government is of god.

Strange...
Didn't the government
Put Jesus to death???

This means that Christians should do whatever the Government says?

Why are they against abortion or same sex marriage?

The government says it's OK.

Didn't they vote?

Just because their guy lost this time;

They agreed to be part of the system by voting.

If you play the game,

Sometimes you lose.

Make lemonade!!!

Are these "Christians" going against the government?

Then they are going against the bible.

They say the bible is the word of god.

Thus,

They are going against god?

As an aside:

Whatever you may think about marriage,

Conventional one man one woman,

Gay marriage,

Transexual marriage,

Multiple partner marriage,

Or any other kind you can imagine;

One thing to remember:

Marriage is a business contract.

It has nothing to do with god.

After all,

You can be married by a judge,

Justice of the Peace, or even a

Ship's Captain (while you are on his ship).

Each state has its own laws regarding marriage;

And divorce:

What happens to the assets if the

Contract is breached?

Which party is at fault?

If both are at fault;

Who is more at fault?

Who gets the children?

Who gets the dog?

It's almost like the dissolution

Of a business partnership.

Because,

That is exactly what it is.

I was married in a church.

During the ceremony,

Myself, my wife,

The best man,

The maid of honor,

And the priest,

All signed the business contract;

I mean, the marriage contract.

Of course, we first had to provide the priest with

The marriage (business) license the government

Had granted us;

For a fee of course.

I knew it!

I knew it!

I knew it!

A few short months after the first

State had passed a law

Legalizing same sex marriage;

The first same sex divorce papers

Were filed!!!

Be careful what you ask for!!!

If you ever have the time,

I recommend reading the bible at least once.

Since my childhood,

I've read it several times.

Different versions.

Not because someone told me to.

But because I was told it was the

Word of God.

You mean God wrote a book?

You better believe I will read it!!!

So, before you criticize my views on the bible;

Maybe you should read it.

Make up your own mind.

Most of it is worthless,

But the first four books of the new testament

Do have good lessons for living life.

At least that's what I have found.

If you don't want to read the whole bible,

Try the first four books of the new testament.

You might get something worthwhile out of it.

Just remember,

The bible is a collection of stories...

Made by man.

I was raised as a Christian.

More particularly, as a Roman Catholic.

I have no religion now.

My beliefs are my own.

As yours should be.

I refuse to have someone else "bind" my mind and body.

In the bible Jesus said,

When you pray,

Go to your room and close the door.

By the way,

Did you know that Catholic means "universal"?

The universal church.

Are all religions going to merge???

Sort of like other corporations do???

For example,

Now we have messianic Jews.

What's another name for a messianic Jew?

Christian???

How can they be both,

Jew and Christian?

Could it be a sign of the times…?

Beginnings of a

Merger???

Mahatma Gandhi once said something to the effect of:

Christians are a beautiful people;

I would really like to meet one.

By the way,

I am not a devotee

Of Gandhi.

But a broken clock is

Right twice a day.

Unless it's a military clock;

Then it's right once a day.

What if the hands fell off?

Then it's always right;

Or always wrong.

Glass half full or half empty?

What if it's a digital clock???

The possibilities are endless.

And for all you Protestants out there,

Who love to criticize Catholics.

Where do you think your religion comes from?

Martin Luther was a Catholic priest/friar

Who became the first protestant,

And started a "competing" religion,

At a time when going against the Catholic church

Meant prison or death?

Somehow he survived.

It sure seems like it was just part of a bigger plan.

Otherwise, the Catholic church would have

Nipped it in the bud.

I'm aware that I tend to criticize "Christians" more than

Others.

That's because it is the religion

I am most familiar with.

And like Gandhi,

I don't think I've ever met a <u>real</u> Christian.

But wait;

For all of those out there of
ALL other religions,
You are also being lied to by your religious leaders,
Books, etc.

I don't discriminate
In my criticism of man-made systems.

The plan began long, long, long ago
To have a united one-world religion.

Same with government.

Have you ever noticed that governments across the
World
Are becoming more aligned with each other?
More standardized?

We will always have separate nations.

Just like in the U.S. we have separate states.

The federal government of the U.S. had very little power
In the beginning.
The states were really like separate nations with a very
Limited federal government.

This changed with the creation of the Civil War.
What about slavery???
Look in the mirror.

Now the federal government is all-powerful
And the states are just submissive, minor governmental
Subdivisions.

At this time we have "independent" nations.
We also have the ineffectual, weak United Nations.

I wonder if a major world war,
A "Civil War" on a global scale,
Could bring about an
All-powerful United Nations?

Then the individual nations

Would become like our states;

Submissive, minor governmental subdivisions.

You don't think it will happen???

Speaking of war…

It's wrong to kill.

Unless the government tells you to.

Do you really think a law or decree can make that OK?

What say you, "Christians"???

In World War II, the major players were the U.S. and Britain against Germany and Japan.

Germany and Japan were bombed into rubble.

Germany and Japan were the losers.

After World War II, the U.S. reconstructed Germany and Japan.
The U.S. paid for this!!!

After World War II,
Germany and Japan became the major
Industrial and manufacturing powerhouses of the world.

Who won???

The main purposes of war
Have always been economic and the consolidation of
Power.
A takeover of territory and the
Serfs attached to it.

Imagine you are a cow.

The farmer makes sure you have good grass,

Hay, and fresh water.

He makes sure you are fenced in

For your protection,

And gives you medicine when you are sick.

You believe that farmer is a nice guy

Because of all he does for you.

Imagine you are a farmer.

Cows = Money!!!

Farmer = Government???

We = Cows!!!

Citizenship is just a legal

Assignment of ownership of a person

To a government who claims the

Right to tax and control that person.

We are chattel!!!

Do you still believe the nations really are

"Independent"???

I have found the secret to understanding

The real reasons for any particular war.

Don't listen to anyone else's opinions.

Just look at the outcome.

You mean they planned it that way???

It seems like anything given to us must have some parts

Of truth to it

So that we end up swallowing the whole thing

Like reasons for war.

Sort of like conspiracy theories.

I have looked into dozens of conspiracy theories.

They all have some good information.

They all have a lot of bad information.

But, mostly they mislead with crazy ideas that bring you

To a pre-determined conclusion.

I wonder if that is done on purpose?

Denial.

Denial.

Denial.

Denial is a river in Egypt.

What???

Remember,

When you look at a map or globe,

North is up and south is down.

Ancient Egypt was divided into upper Egypt and lower
Egypt.

Upper Egypt was to the south.

Lower Egypt was to the north.

Seems counterintuitive?

Not really;

It didn't refer to a map,

But to the current in the river Nile.

Up river was to the south,

Where the river began.

Down river was to the north,

Where the river ended.

The Nile flows northward into the Mediterranean Sea.

Even back then,

Curren(t)cy meant everything.

It is said that Ancient Egypt is the oldest of the great

Civilizations.

We are taught that the Ancient Greek civilization came

After the Ancient Egyptian civilization, and the Ancient

Roman civilization came after the Greeks.

Atlantis is said to have been a mythical civilization

In pre-historic times

That was technologically superior to any

Other known civilizations.

Plato is said to have gotten the idea of Atlantis from his

Grandfather

Who is said to have gotten it from his time spent studying

With the ancient Egyptian priesthood.

Did it really exist?

Actually,

We have no idea how many great civilizations really

Existed in the past;

Or how advanced they may have been.

Perhaps they were destroyed by natural or

Man-made catastrophes.

It is an unexplained fact that man-made artifacts

Have been found embedded in coal

And rock at levels below the surface

Of the earth

That geologists claim are millions

Of years old.

Current science says modern humans are about 300,000

Years old.

Some religions say we are only a few thousand years

Old.

The truth is;

They don't know.

And for those who have studied

Every word of the bible

And have gone through

All the "begats";

And believe you have the timeline down;

Explain this...

How long was it between the first creation of man

And the second creation of man?

Remember in the bible?

God created man,

Male and female he created them.

A little further down it says:

But there was no one to till the soil.

So the lord god created Adam from dirt

And Eve from his rib.

Two separate creations of man???

How long did it take

Between the first and second creation?

Religions just say whatever they want.

Am I picking and choosing only certain passages

From the bible that prove my point?

Of course!!!

That's what all the priests and preachers do.

The difference is that

I don't scare little old ladies out of their

Social security checks

With the threat of eternal damnation.

But science is accurate and exacting.

Isn't it?

That's what my science teachers taught me.

In science there are an hypothesis, a theory, and a fact.

Gravity is a fact.
I agree.

An hypothesis is only a guess made by a scientist.

A theory is only a guess agreed to by two or more
Scientists.

Evolution is a theory.
A guess that is taught as fact.

I agree that there is some type of evolution.

Dogs and wolves evolving
From a common ancestor.
It seems plausible.

But to go from amoeba to human is
Impossible.

To go from ape to human is

Impossible.

On a cellular level and DNA,

Humans are more closely related

To a pig,

Than to an ape.

How did that happen???

I wonder if this has anything to do

With some religions/cultures

Throughout history having rules on

Not eating Pork?

But evolution is proven through the fossil record.

Right???

Forget the fossil record.

Scientists claim to reconstruct how an entire

Species of dinosaur looked and functioned,

Just by finding a piece of a petrified bone.

Remember,

You cannot carbon date rock.

Petrified bone is a rock.

Scientists use conjecture.

"Conjecture" is a fancy way of saying,

"Made up".

If they can use "conjecture" about those things;

Just think what else they "make up".

Therefore,

How reliable is the fossil record

With all that "conjecture" going on?

How did people go from living in tiny tribes,

To forming great, complex civilizations?

A civilization is a man-made system.

It all started because humans are

Lazy by nature.

If you want to do something,

And there is an easy way to do it,

Or a difficult way to do it,

And the results are the same either way;

It only makes sense that the normal person would

Choose the easy way.

Imagine living in a tribe of hunters and gatherers.

Every day is a fight for survival.

Food, water, clothing, shelter.

Every waking minute of every day is spent providing for

Yourself and the others in the tribe.

It's hard work,

But necessary for life.

So,

How do you get out of having to

Do all that hard work?

Make others do it instead!!!

How do you do that?

In the earliest times

Humans yearned for some type of

Consistency in life,

Perhaps for security of mind

And the perceived security of body.

Humans seem to naturally look to someone

Else for answers.

For leadership.

It's scary to realize that you are ultimately

Responsible for yourself.

It's much easier to rely on someone else

Or something else

For protection, leadership…

There was no television, or other distractions
So humans looked to the heavenly bodies;
Sun, moon, and stars.

In a constantly changing life,
The sun, moon, and stars provided a security of mind
In that they were constant.
Their movements were reliable and predictable.
People eventually began to worship these heavenly
Bodies.

This consistency and predictability were first noticed by
Only a few in the tribe.

These few individuals soon figured out that
They could use this knowledge to fool the majority of the
Members of the tribe.

We, the smart ones, will spend our time
Praying to the sun god, moon god, etc.
For continued prosperity of the tribe.

You,

The inferior,

The majority,

Must provide our clothing, food, shelter, etc.

While we are "hard at work";

Praying to the gods,

And performing rituals,

So that the gods don't

Become angry and punish us.

The many on the bottom,

Providing for the few on the top.

A pyramid scheme was born!!!

As an aside:

We humans like to make monuments

Commemorating special achievements.

I wonder why man-made pyramids of many types

Have been found on every continent

Except Antarctica?

Maybe there are even pyramids under the ice.

Pyramids are monuments to the "system"!!!

Furthermore,

Scientists admit that they have no

Evidence that the Great pyramids in Egypt

Were built by the ancient Egyptians.

Slaves working 24/7 for decades

Is just another guess.

Excuse me;

I mean, hypothesis.

No, I mean theory.

It wasn't ET's;

But they may have been built by a more ancient,

More advanced,

Civilization much farther back in history.

There is no telling how long ago the

Pyramid scheme started.

By the way;

In keeping with the times;

Shouldn't they be called

Network Marketing,

Instead of pyramids???

Another aside;

In the old testament,

People would bring their animals to the priests

For sacrifices so that god would forgive them

Of their sins.

The animals were killed, then burned.

The bible says god found the smell of burnt flesh

Appealing.

The animal sacrifices were performed within the walls

Of the sacred temple.

In secret.

Out of sight of the uninitiated.

What do you think the priests were doing with all

Those burnt offerings?

BBQ!!!

These "priests" soon
Realized this was <u>the</u> way to live.
They would perform made-up
Ceremonies, spew some non-sense
Words, sacrifice animals, etc.

So that the sun would be sure to
Rise the next morning
Or for the moon to return, etc.

Ah, the priests/officials had it good.
Servants, slaves, concubines, the finest clothes,
The finest food, finest wine, the finest houses,
The highest social status…
The tribe provided everything
For them
And they did no real work.

Starting to sound familiar???

The priests soon began to

Claim authority over the

Lesser members of the tribe;

And began to rule over them

Both body and mind.

The priests would pass this knowledge

To their sons (suns???) only,

Who would take over

From their fathers,

And so on.

As an aside;

Every time there is a U.S. presidential election coming

up

The news media reports which presidential candidate is
more closely related to

The British royal family.

Yes;

Obama too.

Keep it in the family!!!

This continued on.
The priesthood became
Leaders of the tribe.
Both governmental and religious.
One and the same.

When the tribe would become much larger,
It became too cumbersome to control
Without a division of labor
Among those of the priesthood.

So they came up with the idea of having a
Chief and his men to run the governmental side,
While the religious side was run by the shaman,
Medicine man, priests, etc.

This continues on until today.

The real rulers of the world still control
All governments and religions in order to
Control our mind and body.

As a lengthy aside;

If you have a friend that is a bible thumper,

Don't ever discuss the bible with them,

If you wish to continue being friends.

I tried this once.

Once...

You see,

They will swear on their life

That the Jewish religion came down

From Abraham.

If you read the old testament

You will see that it was

Moses

Who gave the Jews their religion.

Moses…

Said to be the son of a Jewish slave girl, was
Put in a basket in the Nile river
And found by the Pharaoh's daughter
And adopted by her.

So,..

Moses was the adopted grandson
Of the ancient Egyptian Pharaoh…

god on earth.

He grew up in Pharaoh's palace,
Had Jewish servants (slaves),
And was educated by the ancient
Egyptian priesthood.

The bible says he led the Jews out of

Egypt (out of their captivity);

Wandered in the desert for forty years, etc.

Remember,

While Moses was on the mountain

Communing with god and

Receiving the ten commandments;

His people made their own god, of

Go(l)d,

Of course.

You see,

All those years in captivity in Egypt,

The Jews began to confuse their religion

With that of their captors, the ancient Egyptians.

They were "lost".

Moses returned and set them straight.

He claimed to be the only one to commune with god.

Therefore,

The moral of the story;

Moses gave them their religion.

Remember,

Moses was taught the ancient

Egyptian religion from infancy.

In fact,

He got the inside scoop.

You think his education may have had some

Influence on his version of the Jewish religion?

Of course,

This is a story told by humans.

Written much later than it supposedly happened.

Did it really happen?

Who knows???

Remember I'm not picking on a particular religion.

The Christian religion derived from Judaism,

As did the Islamic religion.

Blasphemy!!!

It is an age-old belief that if you know the

Name of a deity,

You can give a command to that deity,

And they must follow it;

If you speak their name.

Three major religions (Judaism, Christianity, and

Islam) follow up their prayers with "Amen".

It is interesting to note "Amen"

(There are various spellings),

Was the chief god of the Ancient Egyptians!!!

I believe in God.

But not like we are taught to.

Like avatars,

Our bodies are biological entities that we inhabit

For a limited time

In order to

Interact with this particular reality.

A bit "out there"?

Imagine being an all-powerful, all-knowing being.

How boring is that!!!

You would probably create countless different "realities"

That operate on different physical laws, etc.

You would even inhabit some of the beings you create

Purposely not giving them memory of who they really are.

So that life would be more interesting.

There is no Hell

There is no Hell

There is no Hell

The concept of hell was created by religions

To control you in this life

By claiming to control the afterlife.

What a crock!!!

Similarly,

There is no karma

There is no karma

There is no karma

How dare I say that!

After all,

Everyone knows that if you do bad things,

Bad things will happen to you in return?

Maybe I don't have a good understanding of karma.

I admit I don't.

But,

I have personally known some of the meanest,

Most selfish, under-handed, back stabbing people you

Can imagine.

Some of them seem to live long, satisfying lives, as

Wealthy people

Who get all the praise from the public.

Sounds like some politicians you know?

Nothing worse happens to them in life,

Then happens to some of the best people.

Where's the karma???

And don't give me that

"In the next life" crap!!!

Remember, <u>ALL</u> religions were created to

Bind your mind and body.

You are a saint

You are a devil

You choose

You take the credit

You take the blame

It's not an outside force

It's You

Do what <u>you</u> believe is right.

Not what someone else says is right.

But, always remember the golden rule.

If you agree with anyone about everything

You are either lying to them

Or lying to yourself.

If you find it necessary to lie to them

In order to "get along";

Such as in the workplace,

Go ahead and lie to them.

If you need the job,

No problem.

But, always

Be true to yourself.

Perhaps the best lesson from

Jesus was the golden rule.

If we all lived by that

The world would be paradise.

I'm no better than you;

I'm a "sinner".

To sin means to miss the mark.

You're not going to hell.

Try to learn from your mistakes.

Try to do better in the future.

Constantly move forward.

Don't beat yourself up for failing.

Everyone misses the mark sometimes.

That's part of being a human being.

Many times in life I came to a crossroads.

Times when I had to make a decision.

Do this.

Or.

Do that.

Right.

Or.

Wrong.

I'm probably 50/50.

That's why I'm just an average guy.

This is why I believe the story of Jesus in the first four

Books of the new testament

Has a lot of meaningful lessons for life.

Whether you believe Jesus was God in human form,

Or just a good man,

Or just a made up story,

The lessons are meaningful.

Once, when being interrogated by the religious leaders of
His day,
Jesus was told he was committing blasphemy by calling
God his father.
Jesus responded by saying,
Is it not written that you are gods?

It has been said that the parents
Live on through their children.

So...

Jesus said God was his father.
He also called everyone his brothers and sisters.
I think this would mean that we are all
God.
Not to be confused with "gods" (remember, there is no "s"
In infinity).
Infinity cannot be subdivided,
Because there is no beginning or end.
God is infinite.

One of the ways our science determines if

Someone is insane

Is if they are having delusions of grandeur.

Believing you are

Napoleon, Caesar, God, etc.

If you don't believe me,

Try telling a psychiatrist or psychologist you are

God.

But they must be correct.

Right???

They have all the education;

Regurgitating things other people have taught them

Onto tests and receiving their

Diplomas,

Certifications from the state, and

Letters after their name.

They are now

Authorized as Authorities.

Now,

Who is delusional???

It seems appropriate that our "authorities" would
Teach this.
After all,
You must believe you are an insignificant
Cog in the wheel of society for this
Civilization to continue to operate.

Otherwise,
You might start to ask:
Why should I do what you say???
Why should I believe what you tell me???
What makes you better than me???

What would have happened to the
Antebellum U.S. economy if all the slaves
Would have banded together and said those things to
Their
Slave masters?

As an aside:

I have many criticisms of education.

Probably more than anything else.

But I am not against education.

In fact,

I believe everyone should learn

As much as they can

About as many different things as they can.

Don't be a one-trick pony.

Some people seem to know everything there is

About a particular subject.

But they know almost nothing about

Everything else.

When I was younger

For a brief time,

I worked as a "technician" in a research lab.

This meant I swept the floors and took out the trash,

Among other things.

Also working there were several physicists and

Chemists,

All were award winning college professors with PhD's

In their field.

Some of them;

I wouldn't let tie my shoes,

Or let near any sharp objects.

I've also known "uneducated"

People that were some of the wisest

People I've ever met.

So, learn as much as you can;

Whether it's a formal education,

Informal,

Or even if you teach yourself.

One way is not necessarily more important than the

Other.

Now,

I don't mean be a "jack of all trades and a master of

None".

Try to master at least one thing in life.

And you do not need a piece of paper

Declaring you have mastered it.

You just need the knowledge for yourself.

Whatever you are learning,

Try to learn it as thoroughly as possible.

I'm not talking about just memorizing;

I mean to really learn it; to

Realize it.

Once you get to the point where you

<u>Real</u>ize something, you will NEVER forget it.

As you go through life,

You will notice that the more varied your

Knowledge base becomes,

The easier it is to learn other things.

Sort of like people who know multiple languages,

Or people who play several musical instruments.

They all say the more they learn, the easier

It becomes to learn more.

School is divided into "subjects".

Life is not.

Everything truly is connected.

For example:

What you learn in chemistry class may later

Help you learn to properly mix paint,

Or decide which chemicals are best

To clean up your mess.

What happens when we die?

Is there an afterlife?

Is it eternal bliss?

Is it eternal suffering?

Is there reincarnation?

Unlike most religions out there,

I won't give you a yes or no answer.

Because I don't KNOW.

They don't KNOW.

But I can tell you what I BELIEVE.

What I guess.

My hypothesis.

Make up your own hypothesis.

It's easy.

Like droplets of rain falling into a sea,

Becoming one again with the

Larger body of water;

We all,

At the end of this physical life,

Join together again

With the larger "body" that is

God.

The only difference between a droplet of water,

And a sea of water,

Is the perceived size.

The constituent parts are the same.

When the droplet joins the larger body,

They are indistinguishable.

They are one.

God is infinite.

Size has no meaning with infinity.

Small = Large.

A Part = The Whole

We are individuals only in this life.

In the afterlife, heaven,

Or whatever you want to name it,

We are one.

God.

God is all powerful.

So anything is possible.

Eternal bliss or suffering?

It's up to you.

Whatever you desire.

But,

It's not a requirement forced upon us

By a greater being.

Why would God create a hell

For eternal suffering as punishment

For breaking certain rules?

If the suffering is for eternity,

We would not have an incentive to

Rehabilitate.

What would be the point?

God is a sadist???

Reincarnation?

Sure,

If you want it.

It's not a requirement.

Come back as a person

In the past, present, or future.

Back and forth.

Anything is possible.

We have all eternity.

Time is only a construct of this reality.

Maybe we sometimes choose to

Relive the same life several times,

Until we "get it right".

Does this explain déjà vu???

What about ESP or a sixth sense?

From my own experiences,

I would say there is something to this.

Sometimes you think of someone

And the phone rings,

And it's that person calling you.

You might be thinking of a particular song,

Then it's next up on the radio.

Sometimes you have a feeling someone you know

Has died or has a serious accident, illness, etc.

You soon find out bad news about a friend or relative.

The examples are almost endless.

What about ghosts?

I don't know.

I do know I have had a couple of strange

Experiences that I can't explain.

I do know that I have had people

That I know and trust tell me about

Experiences they have had.

Since anything is possible;

Maybe there is a totally different type of world

Existing simultaneously to this one.

Occupying the same time and space,

But on a different "frequency".

Maybe our ability to observe this other "frequency" is

Natural to us,

But is conditioned out of us as we grow older.

Maybe sometimes there is a "bleed through" between

These realities.

Maybe that's where children's imaginary friends

Come from.

Scientists continue to find the smallest particles of matter.

No matter how far "down" they go,

They keep finding smaller particles.

These particles are in constant motion

As waves.

In school I was taught that light

Is a wave.

The truth is,

Scientists still cannot determine if light is a

Wave or a particle.

Light seems to exhibit the qualities of

Both.

At the same time.

Sound is a wave.

Sound cannot pass through a vacuum.

Sound requires a medium through which

To pass.

Like air.

Light can pass through a vacuum.

It requires no medium

That we are aware of.

Then,

How can it be a wave?

If light is a particle,

Why doesn't it accumulate?

Visible light is only a small portion

Of the electromagnetic spectrum.

X-rays, gamma rays, etc.

Are also on the EM spectrum.

The EM spectrum is arranged according

To wavelengths of "ra(ys)".

(RA was the ancient Egyptian sun god.)

If the smallest particles of matter

All "vibrate" in a wave-like manner,

Does EVERYTHING act like a wave?

Is EVERYTHING a wave?

The bible says god spoke everything

Into existence.

"Let there be light"

When you speak

You send out sound waves.

Is this a clue as to how this

Universe operates?

Is there a force

Sending out "waves" that

Propagate into the creation

Of all matter that we can

See and touch in <u>this</u> universe?

When we think of something,

Are we sending "thought waves"?

I remember being taught that there were

At least a couple of times in history when two different

People, one not knowing anything about the other,

Living long distances apart;

Tried to get a patent on the same idea

At the same time.

An idea whose time has come???

It seems that young children have this

Ability more than adults.

Maybe it's because as we get older we are

Constantly taught

That such things are not possible.

Just imagine how powerful our minds
Could be if this sense was nurtured
Instead of dismissed.

Maybe we could use this sense
To send out positive thoughts and feelings
To others who are feeling bad.
Maybe we could help others with it.

Maybe there are people in the world who
Have learned to use this ability.

What if some use it for evil?

I have been cursed as being a

Serious person all of my life.

I never thought about how my attitude

Affected others.

I never smiled,

I only spoke when I absolutely had to.

I definitely never made small talk.

I had a negative attitude toward everything.

Several years ago something happened in my own

Life that caused me to take a hard look at myself.

One of the revelations was,

How I looked and acted

Toward other people,

Actually influenced other people's

Attitude and actions toward me.

I began smiling at people more.

When interacting with them, I even started using

Small talk about positive things. Something I had

Never done before.

I began speaking more positively with everyone.

Most importantly, I began <u>thinking</u> more positively.

I noticed instantly that people were nicer to me

And they were much more eager to help, etc.

Especially dealing with clerks at the checkout line.

It's like that old saying that you catch more flies with

Sugar than

Salt.

It really worked and I continued doing it.

Having a more positive, friendlier attitude

Towards everyone and everything.

It now has become "who I am".

Don't misunderstand me.

Life isn't all rainbows and lollypops.

Bad things still happen.

Don't go to the extreme,

And look for just the positive in

Everything.

It is part of our inherit self-preservation mechanism

To see things for what they really are,

Good or bad.

But I've found having a more positive attitude,

Does help you through the tough times.

A negative attitude definitely does not help.

And,

I avoid negative people like the plague.

Why are we here?

I can imagine planting a garden.

I can imagine the plants growing,

Making fruit and vegetables,

Harvesting and eating them.

I can even imagine how they look, feel, smell and taste.

I can even imagine hearing the birds chirping

As I work in the garden.

But there is nothing like the

Actual experience of doing it.

Living the experience.

Taking it in with

All of the senses.

Imagining it can come close,

But there is no substitution for actually

Living it.

Why do people climb mountains?

If you look at it from a "practical" perspective only,

In the end, all they really get is…

To the top.

But sometimes the most important things

Make no "practical" sense at all.

They climb mountains for the experience.

Have you ever noticed how

Young children fight going to sleep?

They want to be awake and aware

Of everything.

They want to experience everything.

Jesus said,

Unless we are like little children

We cannot enter the kingdom of heaven.

Heaven is here.

Living this life.

Living it.

The opposite of living is not death.

Death is just the conclusion of this physical life.

It is part of life.

Just as birth is.

Live spelled backwards is

Evil.

You create your own heaven.

You create your own hell.

You make it happen.

Perhaps the opposite of good (god),

Is the absence of living;

Doing nothing.

So,

Let your light shine.

Burn the candle at both ends.

It's OK.

It's better to burn

Twice as bright for a shorter time,

Than to put your candle under a bed,

And live to an old age.

Adding years to your life seems

Enticing.

But, think about it…

Those added years are always

At the end of your life;

Not the beginning.

Now, I don't mean you shouldn't take care of yourself.

Just don't go to the extreme and

Forget to Live Life.

As I go through life and have different experiences,

The lessons in the first four books of the new testament

Take on different meanings that seem to apply.

Life truly is a journey.

We are constantly changing.

If you are the same person you were a few years ago,

Even a few months ago,

You are not living.

Don't sacrifice

Just for the sake of sacrifice.

You will gain nothing from it.

Unless you sacrifice to help yourself

Or someone else,

You are just denying yourself the pleasures of life.

Live Life.

Love Yourself.

Love Others.

Forgive Others. If they deserve your forgiveness.

Be Positive.

Forgive Yourself.

Sometimes it is best to turn the other cheek.

But, sometimes it is better to come back with a right

Hook.

Choose your battles carefully and wisely.

Remember,

Sometimes what is done,

Cannot be undone.

Just remember what an unknown philosopher once said:

Don't bring a knife to a gunfight!!!

Don't follow leaders.

Be your own.

Be audacious.

(In a good way)

Be unpredictable.

A person who truly thinks for himself is

Unpredictable.

Unpredictable to others in society because

You do not think the way you were

Conditioned to think.

The real rulers of the world are scared to death of

Unpredictable people.

Don't belong to "groups".

You will soon find they expect

You to adopt their beliefs and discard your own.

Like the santa (satan???) clause song says:

Be good for goodness sake.

In other words,

Don't expect to be rewarded for

Doing good.

Just do good.

> *As an aside:*
>
> *Satan is said to be the adversary.*
>
> *The one you must overcome in life.*
>
> *He knows if you've been naughty or nice.*

In the bible Jesus said

When doing charitable works,

Don't let the right hand know

What the left hand is doing.

Don't do good to receive the glory of others.

Do it for your own glory.

The glory you feel inside.

The less other people know about it,

The better.

Be able to stand alone in life.

Knowing what you know.

No matter what others think of you.

It seems that

Most people really don't like themselves.

Do you really expect them to think more of

You than they do of themselves?

Jesus walked to his place of execution

Surrounded by the very people who once supported him,

Who chose him to die when given a choice.

They cursed him and spat on him.

He didn't give in.

He didn't deny what he truly believed.

He didn't defend himself by declaring

The good works he had done.

Even at the cost of his life.

To give in

Would have been to stop moving forward.

At times in your life

You will face criticisms for what you believe.

You will be shunned by friends and family for

Things you do because

You believe they are the right things to do.

You are

And will always be

GOD.

The meaning of life

Is to be

Your own MESSIAH.

NO END

THIS PAGE UNINTENTIONALLY LEFT BLANK

Odds & Ends

bonus radical ramblings of a heretic

In writing this,

I referenced several versions of "God's Word";

Catholic Version,

King James Version,

Gideons Version (free at hotels), and the

New Living Translation Version.

God has been busy!!!

Caution!!: The bible is a collection of stories

Made up by humans.

I'm just giving my interpretation of the

Hidden meanings.

It's my interpretation,

Not my beliefs.

You see there are

Multiple meanings in the bible.

All religions have the "open"

Meanings given to the masses, and

"Esoteric" meanings that the high level priests,

Initiates, etc. teach one another.

These "inner" meanings are not shared with the

Masses of those religions.

In this way,

The masses are able to be controlled.

The God featured at the

Beginning of the book of Genesis

Refers to the Big God.

The God of the creation of this

And any other universes and everything in them.

Typically, this is the God we

All think of when we refer to God.

(I believe we are all God. We are all One.)

What about god everywhere else in the bible?

It is a little "inside joke" that we,

The ordinary people, are not let in on.

If you take a close look at the

Writings in the bible, and

Open your mind,

You will see the Big God created everything;

Then pretty much left it

Alone to operate on its own.

His last creation was man (male and female)

In his image and likeness.

We are told this means

He created them to look like him.

Actually, it means he created them

In the image of his making!

It also does not specify that the

Man he created had a physical body.

God said let us make man in our image.

The plural is used simply to show that

God is not meant to be singular or plural,

But infinity.

You see he created them

Male and female.

In other words,

Just as God is both male and female

(Because he is everything);

So was his creation.

Therefore, man was androgynous

(Both yin and yang).

Another version of God, for want of a better term.

The bible notes that

God rested on the seventh day.

His creation was complete.

After that, the bible starts to call him "Lord" God.

Why the change?

Up to, and including, the

Seventh day of creation,

The bible calls him "God" and after that it changes to

"Lord God".

Remember, God created man,

Male and female (androgynous).

These creatures are the "Lord" gods.

They were created in God's image.

"Lord" is a title of nobility.

"Lord" is not the highest ranking title.

In the feudal system,

A Lord was given control of a

Tract of land by the King or Queen.

Therefore, the "Lord" god was a lesser god.

The "Lord" god was given the

Earth to rule by the Big God;

The main man, the head honcho.

It is the "Lord" god that then

Created Adam from dirt and

Eve from his rib

To till the soil.

It does <u>not</u> mention that

Adam and Eve are in his image or likeness.

Jesus said to the Pharisees that:

You are of your father the devil.

Maybe he was hinting at something?

Lucifer is the "Lord" of this world.

Some say that Satan and Lucifer are the same.

Some say Satan is an agent of Lucifer.

It doesn't matter because it is all just a fairy tale.

Jesus was tempted by the

Devil (Lived spelled backwards)

when put on a high place

And offered the rule of all he could see.

The only way the

Devil could offer this to him was if he,

Himself, had the rule over it in which to give.

The bible is hinting that this

Civilization (system) was created by a little "g" god;

Lucifer/Satan.

I don't have to explain the

Similarity between the words "sun" and "son".

Don't get caught up in the (spell)ing of words.

The pronunciation of words is

More important when tying them together.

In the earliest times the

Sun was worshiped as god.

Since we are all God,

In a patriarchal society,

The male offspring was referred to as "son";

A form of god.

The ancient Egyptians worshiped the

Sun as a god.

The rising sun was equated to

Being in its childhood.

They depicted the young

Sun as a little boy with

His index finger against his chin or lips;

Presumably making the "shhh" sound.

Like we do today to

Signal "quiet" or "secrecy".

The young boy representing the

Newly rising sun was named Horus.

In the morning Horus is rising.

This is where we get the word "horizon".

It is also where we get the word "hour".

In the middle of the day the

Sun or "god" is at his "most high".

As the sun goes down in the evening,

It prepares for its journey through the underworld.

The ancient Egyptian god of the

Underworld was Set.

This is where we get the word "sunset".

Isn't it amazing that some words have been passed
Down from thousands of years ago.

Another interesting word from ancient Egypt is "on".
This is the word they used for the penis.
Today it is still sometimes used to
Describe an erect penis: "hard on".

The concept of the rising sun,
Going to its high point in the sky,
And going down in the west;
Preparing for its journey to the underworld;
And rising again;
Was illustrated by the ancient Egyptians as a
Snake eating its tail (the ouroboros).

Some say this represents reincarnation;
Or maybe endlessness of time; etc.

However, I believe it simply represents "cycles".

Because it seems that cycles are in everything.

(Remember in the bible it says,

There is nothing new under the sun.)

Cycles that are interwoven.

In the bible it refers to

"Wheels within wheels".

It's not referring to a machine;

But to cycles within each other.

The caduceus is the

Symbol used by the medical profession today.

It is two serpents twisted around a staff.

Isn't it peculiar how similar it is to the

Depiction of the double helix of DNA?

But how can that be,

Since this symbol is thousands of

Years old and DNA was

Discovered only within the last century?

We have no idea how old mankind really is,

Or how advanced, civilizations of the

Past may have been.

What was the obsession of the

Upper classes around the

World with bloodlines?

It seems they have always known that

Something in the blood

Would carry down certain

Traits within offspring.

It is an age-old belief by some primitive tribes

That to consume the flesh of your defeated

Enemies was an ultimate form of

Domination.

They believed you were consuming

The essence of that person.

Cain and Abel.

Cain killed Abel.

God could not find Abel. Cain ate Abel.

Cannibal.

The Catholic church teaches that during the

Act of Communion,

Bread and wine are transfigured into the

Body and blood of Christ.

Then...they eat it!!!

Romans Chapter 13:

Do what the government tells you

Because the

"Authorities are appointed by God".

The next time you get a parking ticket,

Remember what god said:

"Thou shalt not park beyond thy

Allotted time;

Unless thou shalt insert another

Dime into thy appointed meter".

We are born into this system.

From the time we are born

We are expected to obey all

Laws that are already in existence.

I thought we have a

Say in how our government works?

You are not eligible to vote until you are 18.

But you are required to obey

Laws that were implemented

Before you were eligible to vote;

Even before you were born?

I quit voting many years ago.

I never will again.

I refuse to give anyone authority over myself.

What about laws that were

Passed since I quit voting?

Am I required to do what the

"Authorities" tell me just because I am a

Citizen?

I guess I'm a citizen.

No one ever asked me to be a citizen.

I never gave an oath to be a citizen.

All I know is I was born in and

Lived in the U.S. all of my life.

I have been told I am a U.S. citizen.

I have never renounced my citizenship.

So...

I guess I am a U.S. citizen.

But just because I am a citizen,

Does that mean I automatically

Must follow whatever the

Government tells me?

I guess

Plymouth Rock really did land on me!!!

I believe that you are culpable for

Breaking laws no matter when

They were passed, if you continue voting.

You are "in the game" when you

Agree to vote.

Whether what or whom you vote for wins or loses,

It doesn't matter.

Your participation means you

Agree to play the game.

When you play a game

You must agree to the rules;

Whether the outcome is in your favor or not.

If you play the game

You must accept the consequences.

But what if I purposely

Refuse to continue to vote?

Am I saying I no longer want to

Play the game and the

Rules no longer apply to me?

Now, I'm not one of those

"Sovereign citizens" that believe

They can get out of obeying laws

By some legal trickery.

You can't beat their game by

Playing their game.

And I'm not even interested in

"Getting out of" following the law.

My argument is purely philosophical;

But also a matter of principle.

You see I understand that some

Laws are necessary when living in a

Civilization such as ours.

You can't allow people to go

Around raping and pillaging.

There must be consequences for bad behavior.

However, what about laws against people's actions

that do not cause harm to anyone?

If I go over the speed limit and

Cause no accident;

Why do I have to pay a fine?

I didn't cause any harm to anyone.

I know... Just do as you're told and shut up!!!

After all it's a slippery slope.

Today it's speeding; tomorrow it's

Mass murder!!!

So... Anyway...

I try to follow the law as best I can.

(I still speed sometimes)

It's usually more of a hassle to

Break the law and try to get away with it,

Then it is to just follow it in the first place.

Ask anyone in prison.

By the way;

If you really want to piss off cops,

Obey all the traffic laws.

After all,

If they can't meet their quota of tickets,

They get reprimanded.

And don't give me that "there are no quotas" crap!!!

A quota by any other name is still a quota.

The point I'm trying to get to is that

I follow the laws imposed on me out of duress.

All laws.

You see I quit participating in the system by

Consciously not voting.

So I follow the laws under threat of

Injury to my body and/or property.

My body is injured if I have my freedoms restricted.

My property is injured if I have to pay a

Fine or penalty.

If I am called to court to testify,

I will do so truthfully.

I will even swear an oath to tell the truth.

You see I'm doing so under duress.

But I'll still do it because I don't

Want to go to jail for

Contempt of court or perjury.

By the way...

In the bible Jesus said

"Swear no oaths"

Just answer truthfully.

Why do I see all these

"Christians" swearing an oath before

Testifying in court?

And they do it with their hand on a bible!!!

I guess they never read it.

Surprise, Surprise!!!

The reason they make you swear an

Oath to tell the truth is so

They can accuse you of perjury if you lie.

You see they set the rules of the

Game before you testify.

If you break the rules,

You go to jail.

Court is a very curious thing

If you look at it from an esoteric perspective.

Before the "priest" walks in,

Everyone must rise.

The "priest" walks in dressed in a black robe.

He steps behind an altar (he is altered).

He sits. Now everyone else can sit.

This "priest" represents Saturn/Satan.

He is the adversary;

The opposer.

He is the one you must overcome.

If you are accused of a crime,

He tells you the charges being

Brought against you.

He asks if you "understand" the charges.

He does <u>not</u> ask if you

"Comprehend" the charges.

To comprehend is to know the

Meaning of something.

To "understand" means you agree to

"Stand under" the charges against you.

It means you agree to all the

Laws backing the charges and to the

Authority of the court.

It's like when you sign a contract to purchase a

House or car, etc.

Near the place for your signature

It will say that you have read,

Understand and agree to all the

Terms of the contract.

No one can <u>comprehend</u> that contract!

It's written by dozens of lawyers

Who are all experts in contract law.

You see, it doesn't matter

Whether or not you comprehend it.

All that matters is that you

Understand "stand under" the

Terms of the contract.

As the defendant

You may have a lawyer represent you or

You can appear "pro se",

Which means you represent yourself.

"Pro se" is Latin for "for himself".

Another Latin term is "cutis".

This means "skin".

It is the root word of "cuticle" like on a fingernail.

The suffix "or" means one who does, etc.

You see,

In their legalistic logic,

The controllers of this world

Know that you (and everyone else) is God.

They know you are a sovereign.

You see Kings and Queens (sovereigns)

Are, and always have been, above the law.

They have no peers in their country,

Therefore, they can never be tried for a

Crime under the legal system of their country.

Similarly, since you are God,

They believe that only you can accuse

Yourself of a crime.

Therefore, the defendant can appear

"Pro se";

and he is accused by the opponent

Which is a person appearing in "his skin";

That is, in the skin of the defendant.

Confused yet?

That person is called the

"Pro se cutor"

(For himself – one who is the skin)

Or as it is spelled in English;

"Prosecutor"!!!

So...

You are actually accusing

Yourself of a crime.

Did you know that???

Each side makes their

Plea to the judge (Satan).

They argue their case to the judge,

Not to each other.

Each side tries to

Overcome the judge (Satan).

The judge makes the

Ruling for one side or the other.

Juries only provide a verdict;

The judge rules anyway he wants

No matter what the jury says.

Don't believe me?

Ask a lawyer if a judge can

"Set Aside" a jury verdict.

So...

One side wins;

The other loses.

Court is adjourned and

"All rise" is cried out as the judge stands up.

Everyone stands up.

Once he exits the court,

Everyone can sit, or whatever.

Every day courts are in session,

This scenario plays out hundreds of times,

Maybe more, all over the country

(And the world).

And only an extreme

Few of the observers or participants

Realize they are taking part in an

Age-old religious ceremony.

This is not taught in law school.

Did you ever think about why you

Pay fees to the government?

For instance,

If you own a piece of property

And decide to build a house on it,

You must pay a fee to the local government

To obtain permission to build the house.

On your own property!

What did the government do to earn that money?

It is your land.

You are paying for the house yourself.

Why should the government make a

Profit from this?

In some locales this fee

Is a percentage of the building cost

And the fee may be in the

Thousands of dollars.

A fee for a license to be married???
Explain that one!!!

What about paying a fine
For speeding?

Government charging fines, fees, and penalties
Is like creating money from nothing.

Remember, the local government is already
Being funded by your property taxes and
Sales taxes!!!

Fines, fees, and penalties are just the icing on
Their cake.

Same thing with donations to religions.

Government and religions

Have always been the largest money

Making scams throughout history.

Their main function is to control you.

But it's nice to have that added feature

For a few of the minions in charge

To make money from nothing.

If you own a business,

Wouldn't it be nice to be able to collect

Money for doing nothing?

Especially if the law required it?

Backed up by someone with a badge and gun?

It's all PURE PROFIT!!!

I think these organizations

Should all be audited regularly and

Have all of their actions

Closely scrutinized.

I'm sure they all have people

Taking a little for themselves.

It has to be.

There is too much money involved

For people not to be tempted.

And while I'm on the subject;

NON-PROFIT "charitable" organizations are also

SCAMS!!!

I often wondered about these "donations".

You know, organized crime is always on the

Look out for ways to launder money.

All that unaccounted for cash

Coming in as donations, "no questions asked".

TAX FREE!!!

Religions and non-profit organizations

Are a money launderer's dream.

Have you noticed all the new

Non-profit charities and churches

Popping up all over???

With their leaders driving expensive

Luxury cars and living in expensive

Houses?

So...

They say;

The god of this world is Lucifer.

He created this civilization.

He controls this civilization.

He believes

"Bad" is as necessary as "good".

There must be a

Negative to have a positive.

There must be a black to have a white.

Let me be clear.

Most of the people that believe

Lucifer (and/or Satan)

Rule this world are not like the

"Satan Worshippers" as presented in the

Media/Hollywood.

They don't believe in a

Devil with horns and a tail, etc.

They don't necessarily

Desire evil or bad things to happen.

They believe that the only

Way we can have good in the

World is to also have evil.

They believe there is a natural balance.

This does

Not necessarily mean they are

Bad people.

Not necessarily.

The floor in the temple areas of

Masonic lodges are

Black and white checkerboard designs.

This is to symbolize the need for

Opposing forces in this civilization.

Sort of like the yin-yang symbol.

In the middle of the

Masonic temple is an altar.

Placed on top of this

Altar is a religious book.

It is usually a book of the

Religion of the majority of the

Members of that lodge.

The Masons do not care what

Religion you follow.

(Remember the Masons are located in

Every country of the world).

But they do

Require you to belong to a religion.

You see,

They know all religions are

Controlled by the

Real rulers of the world.

So, as long as you belong to a religion,

You are eligible to be a member.

They know you have been

Conditioned to follow the system.

The altar is always facing the east.

It is where the sun rises.

On the east side of the temple sits the

Grand Master of that Lodge.

During ceremonies,

The members may sit along

Any wall of the temple,

Except along the wall to the north.

(The Masons say the

North represents darkness.

They are all about light.

Lucifer represents light.

There are parts of the world in the

Northern hemisphere,

To the extreme north that are in

Total darkness during the winter.)

So, no one sits on the north side...

Except during the ceremony to raise a

Mason to the third degree,

Which is the Master Mason degree.

During that ceremony there is a

Curious character sitting on the

North side (He lives in the North Pole).

He is dressed in red with white trim

And wears a white wig and beard.

This character asks many intrusive

Questions of the candidate.

In order to have the

Master Mason title bestowed upon him,

The candidate must go through the

Third degree and overcome the

Opposer/adversary,

Who is the fellow dressed in red and white.

He is called by many names:

The old man of the north, old scratch, old nick,

Saint Nick, Saint Nicholas,

Santa Clause…. Satan.

On every Masonic lodge there is

A plaque or stone with writing.

It has the date of the sanctification of that

Lodge in two dates.

The first date is followed by A.D.,

Which is the normal way the

Western world dates years since the

Time of Jesus (anno domino – year of our lord).

The second date is

4,000 years previous and is

Followed by A.L.,

Which stands for anno Lucifer

(The year of Lucifer).

This is supposedly when

Lucifer gave the light (knowledge)

To humanity

(You know, the knowledge of

Good and evil – remember

Black and white checkerboard).

The real rulers of the world have

Never gone away.

Not since they began ruling others in

Primitive times until the present day.

(This may have started millions of years ago;

Who knows?)

Their descendants were taught the

Secrets of controlling the masses

And they continue to pass this

Knowledge on to their offspring until this day.

They have never been "taken over";

They have never been "defeated";

They have never "fallen".

They don't believe the religions they give people.

They know all humans are God.

They try to keep this a secret.

They want everyone else to think of

Themselves as being

Inferior so that they are more easily controlled.

They never give up their power.

(Do you really think they would let

The little people like us actually control

"Our" own country???)

We are told that great civilizations rise and fall.

That is not correct.

Great civilizations rise and are

Relocated and altered,

Leaving behind a complete system in

Control of a territory of land and people;

With the constant goal of spreading

Over the entire world in order to

Control the entire globe and

Everyone and everything on it.

I'm not talking about the

Lower level rulers such as Kings, Queens,

Caesars, etc.

I mean the real rulers behind the scenes that

Control the controllers.

The names we have never known

And never will know.

Great catastrophes have occurred over

This long time span.

Some were natural, some man-made.

Such catastrophes caused the

Real rulers to "start all over again".

That is why after all this time

They are just now realizing total global control.

They had done it in the past.

Maybe many times.

But catastrophes would cause them to re-start.

Scientists have found Egyptian mummies

Dating back to the time of the Pharaohs

That have red/blonde hair.

These were mummies of very high social status.

You see, the real rulers of ancient

Egypt were not the same race as the

Indigenous people of Egypt.

They are depicted in paintings, bas reliefs,

And statues as having elaborate headdresses

And/or wearing wigs.

I was taught in school that they

Wore wigs because they shaved their heads

Due to a problem with lice.

This makes no sense.

Remember, these were Pharaohs, high priests,

And their families.

Do you really think they had a problem with lice?

They had servants to do everything for them,

Including bathing them.

Servants would even clean their bottom

After they used the bathroom.

They didn't have to lift a finger for anything.

A lice problem???

No, the reason they were depicted

With wigs was to make them seem

More like the indigenous people of Egypt,

Who have dark hair.

They probably did wear wigs when they

Made public appearances.

But their real hair was still there and was

Red and/or blonde.

Their servants most certainly knew

Their real hair color.

But, they knew better than to reveal such secrets.

They knew that severe punishment,

Maybe even death, would be waiting for them.

Anyway,

What is the big deal about hair color?

Well, it is to illustrate that the

Real rulers were not the same as the

Indigenous people,

But they fooled them into thinking

They were the same.

The real rulers of ancient

Egypt didn't just die off along with the

"Fall of the Egyptian Civilization".

In fact the ancient Egyptian Civilization

Did not fall at all.

The real rulers just kept moving farther

West to set up other civilizations to

Continue their march to global control;

While leaving the previous empire under the

Control of their minions.

Remember,

Cleopatra was a descendant of the Ptolemy line.

Ptolemy was a Greek who declared himself

Pharoah of Egypt.

The next great civilization to come was the

Greek Civilization.

Supposedly they invented "democracy".

Ha, Ha, Ha, Ha...

After the Greek Civilization came the

Roman Civilization.

It was the same real rulers

Behind the scenes that just

Kept moving westward.

The ancient Romans even "copied" the

Greek architecture.

Their governments were also structured similarly.

They even had the same

Pantheon of gods (just the names changed).

The ancient Roman Civilization didn't fall.

The eastern portion of the empire in the

Middle east just continued to rule that area

(And eventually created the Islamic religion).

The western portion of the empire

Morphed into the Roman Catholic Church.

Caesar became the Pope;

The Senate became the Cardinals;

The priesthood and high level

Administrators became the new priesthood

(Roman Catholic priests at that time

Could marry and have children);

Monks stayed monks;

And the priestesses of

Goddesses like Vesta (Vestal Virgins)

Became nuns.

The pantheon of gods became the twelve apostles

And the saints.

Jesus became the Christ figure

Which goes back to previous

Religions in history.

The God figure was taken from the Jewish religion
(Which actually came from Moses who was
Educated by the ancient Egyptian priesthood).

The steady move westward continued
Into Europe.

The Kings and Queens of Europe were all
Crowned by the Pope.

Other Christian religions were created.

The "New World" was conquered and the
Western hemisphere was colonized by
European Christians.

In more modern times we have the

Tidying up of the mergers of nations.

World War II put the final nail in the coffin.

The world became standardized.

Don't be fooled by things like the "wars" we have

Had since WWII.

These are just to "fine tune" the mergers.

And don't be fooled by the Cold War and

The Communist Threat.

If the Soviet Union was such an

Enemy of the "Democratic" nations,

Why did the U.S. provide humanitarian

And financial aid to the Soviet Union and

China all those years?

Does it make sense to aid your enemies?

Watching the news when I was growing

Up was scary.

They would show these graphs of

All the nuclear missiles the Soviet Union had

Compared to the U.S.

The Soviets outnumbered the U.S. by far.

Doesn't it seem like the U.S. should

Have stopped giving aid to the USSR

So that they would have to spend their own

Money on food instead of weapons???

I was just a kid

And I could figure that out!!!

You see,

The world is not at all the way

It has been portrayed to us.

Out of World War II the USSR

Became a world super power,

As it was intended to be.

The USSR expanded by conquering

Territories during and after WWII.

You see, these were all small independent

Countries in eastern Europe.

The quickest way to consolidate them

Was to have a Super Power

Simply take them over.

This was intentionally done by the

Rulers of the world on their continuing

March to consolidate all nations of the world.

Have you ever heard the

Talking heads on news programs

Mention "The American Experiment"?

Well, it is just that,

An experiment.

So was communism.

So is socialism.

In the end,

We will be given a "system"

Which will be an amalgamation

Of Capitalism, Socialism, Fascism, and Communism.

Out of all of these "Experiments"

The real rulers of the world have

Found the different parts of each

System that will work for them

In the coming future One World Government.

So, how will it happen?

What will it look like?

There will be a major world war in the future.

When?

I don't know.

But it will be needed to bring about the final

One World Government/Religion.

I know what you are thinking.

If the real rulers of the world are so united,

And so powerful;

What is the need for having wars?

Can't they just make the changes

They want, happen?

Well,

Think of the leaders of nations, high level

Politicians and bureaucrats

As being managers;

Because that is what they really are.

They receive the tasks given by the real rulers

And they make sure they are implemented.

Ask a manager of a store or restaurant,

Who manages a handful of employees,

How difficult it is to make them do their jobs.

Now imagine managing a few BILLION employees.

It has been said that more changes

Can be made in a couple of years of war,

Then in 20 years of peace.

So,

War is needed to make difficult,

But necessary changes take place

Relatively quickly.

War also has the added "benefit"

Of population reduction.

Besides war, there is a major campaign,

Which is needed to bring about change in

Human behavior, that

Has been raging for many years and continues to

Intensify more and more.

Climate Change!!!

In the 1970's the fearmongers would terrify us

With dire predictions of Global Cooling.

More recently it was Global Warming.

However, the data didn't always match

Their version of reality

So now they call it a catchall term,

Climate Change!

Big Surprise!!!

The climate has always changed.

Cooling periods,

Warming periods,

Melting ice,

Rising seas,

Expanding of glaciers,

Falling seas.

So what is their reason for

This climate change hysteria?

It's Our Fault!!!

"We humans are a blight on this planet

That must be eradicated."

You see,

The real rulers of the world don't need

So many of us anymore.

They needed us in order to advance civilization

To the point that supported the

Development of technology that

Allowed them to extend their physical

Lives indefinitely.

They have reached that point.

Now its time to "cull the herd".

They probably only need about

5% of the population,

When its all said and done.

<u>Someone</u> has to do the work for them.

This sounds far-fetched, I know.

But this is the only explanation that makes sense.

Now, when I say they can extend their lives

Indefinitely,

I don't mean they can live forever.

I mean that at <u>their</u> current level of technology,

They can extend their lives for many,

Many more years.

It is an ongoing process.

Let's say they can now extend their lives

For another 200 years.

Since their current technology can do this,

It only makes since that within another 100

Years or so, they may improve the technology

To add another 200 years,

And so on....

The world they yearn for is one

Without all of us little people.

They envision a world of peace and harmony

With nature.

All natural foods, clothing, etc.

Wild animals romping through the forests.

No more cities.

No more pollution.

It sounds like paradise doesn't it?

The only problem is little people like

Us don't have a place in their

World of the future.

Just the few of them on the top,

With about 5% of us to do the work

For them on the bottom.